T0039244

AN INEXCUSABLE ABSENCE

The Shortage of Black Male Teachers

R. Perez Gatling, M.Ed.
Veleka S. Gatling, Ph.D.
Leroy Hamilton, Jr., Ed.D.

authorHOUSE®

AuthorHouse™ LLC
1663 Liberty Drive
Bloomington, IN 47403
www.authorhouse.com
Phone: 1-800-839-8640

Published by AuthorHouse   05/29/2014

ISBN: 978-1-4918-3918-8 (sc)
ISBN: 978-1-4918-3919-5 (e)

Library of Congress Control Number: 2013921796

Special thanks to Russell Gatling, Cleo Gatling, Leo V. Williams, Jr., Carolyn L.S. Williams, Leroy Hamilton, Sr., (the late) Gloria I. Hamilton, and Erica Hamilton, and Sierran Upton, and Annie S. Perkins

CONTENTS

Introduction.. ix

A Brief History of African Americans
and Education.. xv

Statistical Data Regarding the Number
of Black Male Teachers... xix

Chapter 1   Why Don't People (in General)
             Want to go into Education?......................... 1
Chapter 2   Why Don't More Black Men
             Choose to go into Teaching?..................... 13
Chapter 3   Why Should African American Men
             Choose Teaching as a Career?..................18
Chapter 4   Role Models... 42
Chapter 5   The Contemporary Black Teacher
             as a Role Model for Black Boys.................55
Chapter 6   On the Front Lines.................................... 68
Chapter 7   Historical Black Teachers and Scholars... 73
Chapter 8   Profiles of Men in Education 87

Conclusion...101
Works Cited...105

Introduction

If one were to produce a documentary on educators, administrators, and schools in general, one would assuredly see certain things (no matter what school district one chose to observe). One would see principals struggling to unify a body of students and teachers as diverse as seashells on the beach (some successfully, others . . . not so much). One would see the upwardly mobile, ambitious administrator who has impressed everyone at central office and is destined to be a principal (if he or she is not already one) or a superintendent. In many cases, this single-minded, motivated individual burns the candle at both ends in an effort to make a good impression on his or her supervisors. It is not unusual to see this individual at school in the evening or on weekends. It is also not unusual to see the over-achiever at school board meetings and other gatherings where there are people of power and influence. Unfortunately, there is also the assistant principal who has lost all hope of ever becoming a principal because he or she has been passed over so many times. There is also the idealist who went into teaching with the idea that he or she could change the world but has been jaded over the years because he or she feels that the children aren't like they used to be, the system is flawed and will never change, and the rigid nature of education today is counterproductive to the liberty that exists in true knowledge and erudition. Finally, there is the teacher who has assuredly found his or her calling. This individual enjoys coming to work each day, and he or she puts up with the bureaucracy in exchange for the joy and unparalleled satisfaction associated with helping young people.

The filmmaker could also chronicle the exploits of the person in the classroom who had aspirations of running a Fortune 500 company but has "settled" for teaching. What a bummer! That person thought he or she would do so much more with his or her life. There are also educators who have worked for large companies but didn't find the intrinsic satisfaction they thought they would and ended up teaching. Let us not forget the retired educators who remember when teaching was a respected profession, and they proudly profess their love and regard for the line of work they chose and the students whose lives they touched.

As far as students go, there are students who come to school for peace and safety because there is none at home . . . and students who are determined to be the first in the family to graduate from high school. Let's not forget the students who never come to school because (pick one):

a.   they say they do not care about school, but (in actuality) they do not have the skills that are necessary to succeed,

b.   they have to babysit a younger brother or sister or a child of their own,

c.   they have an older girlfriend or boyfriend who encourages them to skip school to play house,

d.   they feel insecure and are afraid that no one will like them, or they are afraid of a bully or a group of bullies.

As far as the students who come to school regularly, there is the "typical" student. By typical, we are not referring to the student's abilities or even the student's potential for success, but the characteristics he or she possesses that are comparable to most students in America. This student works hard, does not cause a lot of trouble, is obedient, and rolls with the punches hoping that God or karma will recognize his or her goodness and reward him or her with goodness and peace. This student is often ignored because he or she is generally a self-starter and gets along pretty well without an overabundance of assistance from the teacher. There is also the high achiever. This student is driven, competitive, and focused. In some cases, the high achiever has conscientious or overbearing support at home from parents or guardians who will accept nothing less than stellar marks and high class rankings. Some high achievers do not have a strong support system at home and are more intrinsically motivated.

These (and countless other) forces, spirits, experiences, and peoples connect 180 plus days each year to form an organization that is supposed to be a microcosm of the real world . . . a school. The ranks of educators in this real-world model are devoid of one group in large or even respectable numbers . . . Black men. Some people may say: "Oh, no! Not another book about blackness and how unfortunate the Black boys in our society are and how Black boys and Black men are in the most piteous and painful of predicaments!" This is not that book. (That may be the next book.) This book is about the scarcity of Black male educators. Those of us who work in education are well aware of the paltry number of Black men in the classroom, as well as the overwhelming need for them on various levels. People should not be surprised to see thorough, articulate, Black men in front of the classroom educating our young people; it should be the rule more than the exception. It is inconceivable to think that our social, educational, and civil rights pioneers campaigned, remonstrated, suffered, and endured unspeakable privations and hardships only to have the African Americans of the present generation desecrate the victories of the past through laziness and apathy. Educated Black men should be well represented in all professions, especially education. This is where the seeds are sown and the foundation is laid for the next generation of lawyers, doctors, social workers, bankers, politicians, business owners, and yes, educators.

A Brief History of African Americans and Education

Very few Blacks received any education at all until public schools were established during the Reconstruction. In the early 1950's, racial segregation was the norm in the "United" States. Although White children and Black children did not attend the same schools, the overarching idea was that the schools for each were supposed to be equal . . . separate, but equal. The reality was that most Black schools were far inferior to their White counterparts. In Topeka, Kansas, a Black third-grader named Linda Brown had to walk one mile through a railroad switchyard to get to school, even though a White elementary school was only seven blocks away. The young lady's father, Oliver Brown, tried to enroll her in the White elementary school, but the principal of the school turned them down. Brown sought help from McKinley Burnett, the head of Topeka's branch of the NAACP. Other Black parents joined Brown, and in 1951, the NAACP requested an injunction that would forbid segregation in Topeka's public schools (Cozzens, 1998).

A verdict was handed down after more than two years of hearings, motions, injunctions, and appeals. Chief Justice, Earl Warren, read the decision of the unanimous Court:

> We come then to the question presented: Does segregation of children in public schools on the basis of race, even though the physical facilities and other 'tangible' factors may be equal, deprive the children of the minority group of equal opportunities? We believe that it does . . . We conclude that in the field of public education the doctrine of '"separate but equal"' has no place. Separate educational

facilities are inherently unequal. Therefore, we hold the plaintiffs and others similarly situated for whom the actions have been brought are, by reason of the segregation complained of, deprived of the equal protection of the laws guaranteed by the Fourteenth Amendment.

The Supreme Court struck down the 'separate but equal' doctrine of *Plessy* for public education, ruled in favor of the plaintiffs, and required the desegregation of schools across America.

One would have thought that segregation ended at that point, but just like the case with slavery, the practice of segregation did not end when the law was passed. According to Reber (2005), little progress was made during the decade following the Supreme Court's decision. The first generation of desegregation plans of the late 1950's and the early 1960's facilitated the move of just a handful of Black students to White schools or allowed for "voluntary transfers" to different schools, which produced only miniscule reductions in segregation. The large-scale, court-ordered plans were mostly imposed following a series of Supreme Court rulings between 1968 and 1971.

STATISTICAL DATA REGARDING THE NUMBER OF BLACK MALE TEACHERS

Today, most public schools in America are desegregated, but every population is not represented in the pool of faculty. Black men are underrepresented in the field of education, and there have been a number of research studies conducted within the last decade that substantiate this. A survey conducted by the National Education Association (NEA) in 2004 revealed that the number of male public school teachers was at its lowest point in 40 years. Only 21% of the nation's three million teachers were men. When broken down by race, the numbers are even more alarming. Black male teachers made up only 16% of the teaching population, and almost 42% of public schools had no minority teachers at all. According to former NEA President, Reg Weaver (who happens to be African American), "The sad reality is that a young boy could go through his entire education without ever having a teacher who looks like me" (Toppo, 2003). According to Dr. Roy Jones of the Call Me MISTER Program, a program dedicated to recruiting and retaining Black male teachers, of the more than 20,000 teachers in South Carolina, Black males represent only one percent (Lewis, 2005). The recent statistics are even more startling. "While 35% of the nation's public school students are Black or Latino, less than 15% of the teachers are Black or Latino." Of that 15%, only 2% are Black men (Diamond, 2011). In terms of the number of Black men enrolled in teacher preparatory programs, only 1% of the students enrolled in teacher preparatory programs are Black men (Milloy, 2013).

The dearth of Black male teachers prompted U.S. Secretary of Education, Arne Duncan, and filmmaker, Spike Lee, to join forces to urge more Black men to consider entering the teaching profession. This was a bold and unprecedented call to action. "More than 1 million teachers will retire during the next decade, according to federal estimates, and leaders have embarked on a drive to build a more diverse teaching force." Duncan took his campaign to Atlanta's historic, all-male, Morehouse College in January 2011. In his address, Duncan asserted, "Teachers should look more like the people they serve" (Diamond, 2011).

CHAPTER 1

Why Don't People (in General) Want to go into Education?

Perception of the Profession

Now-a-days, people want to be a part of what people used to call the "jet set." In today's lingo, it is called living a "Champagne Life." Living a "Champagne Life" involves driving big SUV's or luxury sedans with heated leather seats, GPS's (that are rarely used), satellite radios, and DVD players. It involves owning a wardrobe comparable to that of a movie star, and having enough money to eat dinner out every night and lunch out every day, and enough cash to take lavish, extended-day cruises and vacations to exotic locales. Young and people old people alike graduate from college expecting to be rich psychologists, sociologists, actors, doctors, lawyers, pediatricians, technology gurus, business owners, and music producers. There is not much fanfare when scholars (young and old) announce that they desire to be educators. If high school seniors were surveyed, many would say that there is no way on God's green Earth . . . no friggin' way . . . no way in the world, that they would graduate and become . . . **teachers.** As a matter of fact**,** if one were to take a sneak peak at exit surveys and career inventories that juniors and seniors complete for their guidance counselors, one might find that teaching is pretty low on the list of careers chosen by most students.

Let's face it; teaching is not glamorous, prestigious (although it should be), or even cool, for the most part! One never sees a teacher on one of those popular reality shows talking on the cell phone in the back of a limo or in a convertible making million dollar deals. In the new millennium, when people think of teachers, they think of marginally successful, miserable, broke, meek, quasi blue collar wretches charged with holding America's restless youth at bay and "entertaining" them while their parents, who have "important jobs," are out there saving the world.

In terms of what politicians have had to say about public education in the last 10 years, it seems as if their mantra has been "America's public schools are failing our children." Newspapers, magazines, and television news programs have been riddled with stories about the following:

- low test scores
- high dropout rates
- disgruntled parents
- disgruntled students
- disgruntled teachers
- incompetent leaders
- inadequate educational funding
- low teacher salaries
- guns and violence in schools
- appalling student behavior
- laughable resources
- cheating on standardized tests

Issues like these cast a negative light on public education.

<u>Bad Kids/Powerless Teachers</u>

Yet another reason why people do not go into education is the perception that children are "bad." We all remember the "class clown" who kept his or her peers in stitches and kept the teacher from teaching. This was the same kid who always had a smart comment for the teacher when he or she was asked a question. We remember the kid who always challenged the teacher's authority, as well as the one who was smart but chose to use his intelligence to be a wise guy. We remember the students who banded together to make sure that nothing productive occurred while they were in class. These students knew that they had no intentions of allowing the teacher to provide any instruction, and they made a concerted effort to disrupt the class, keep the teacher on the defensive, and utterly destroy the teacher's credibility, self-esteem, and in some cases, his or her career. If we are truthful with ourselves, some of us enjoyed the distraction that these students provided.

People also see schools (especially urban schools) as violent places. These people who view schools as violent places base their opinions on statistics published by various political factions, as well as other groups committed to exposing the worst side of public schools in an effort to convince the government to subsidize their children's private-school tuition. (That is another story.) In many cases, believe it or not, members of the media even sensationalize stories about students and schools.

There have also been numerous movies in which a teacher's attempt to bring an incorrigible class of nefarious teenage students under subjection is the focus. Many of these movies depict teachers as weak, soft-spoken, mousy, laughable individuals who have their dreams of changing the world dashed by disrespectful, unruly, uncaring miscreants who couldn't care less about education, teachers, or adults in general. What a way to depict educators! Lots of people choose not go into education because of the discipline problems that they think most teachers have with most students. The recurring statement is "I admire you. I couldn't be a teacher because I would kill somebody's child." Of course, we know these people don't mean it literally, but their perception is that there is an overall lack of discipline in the public schools.

<u>Money</u>

According to Stan Jones, a professor at the University of Alabama, "There is no doubt that low salaries are the main evidence for the low professional status of teachers, and I agree wholeheartedly that raising salaries is the most important step we can make in attracting more competent teachers to the schools:" (Jones, ed., n.d.).

> Anemic growth in teacher salaries is making it increasingly difficult for teachers, especially new ones, to find affordable housing in their communities and to pay off student loan debts, according to the latest teacher salary survey released by the American Federation of Teachers (AFT). These and other factors place the teaching profession-already plagued by high turnover and recruiting challenges-in further peril. The AFT report asserts that, to make teacher pay competitive with other professions by the end of the decade, teachers need a 30% raise-an additional investment in our

children's future of almost $15 billion per year.

According to the same article, teacher raises fell short of the annual rate of inflation in 2004-2005. "Between 2003 and 2005, the buying power of the average teacher salary decreased by almost $800" (2007). Although the AFT's "Survey and Analysis of Teacher Salary Trends 2007" reported that the salary increase in 2007 was the highest in 15 years, teachers still only earn about 70 cents on the dollar compared to similar professionals.

Teacher Satisfaction

Teacher job satisfaction is associated with work performance, including teachers' involvement, commitment, and motivation on the job (Sargent & Hannum, 2005). What is "job satisfaction?" Job satisfaction is the degree to which people like the aspects of their jobs (Spector, 1997). Job satisfaction is connected to performance, productivity, absenteeism, turnover, task success, professional attitude, and other social and personal variables (Iaffaldano & Muchinsky, 1985; Levinson, Fetchkan, & Hohenshil, 1988). The study of job satisfaction can be traced to the Hawthorne studies conducted during the late 1920s (Landsberger, 1979). Studies of job satisfaction also emerged in the 1970s (VanVoorhis & Levinson, 2006).

Schools are losing qualified teachers because of low job satisfaction (Grose, 2006). Factors of dissatisfaction encompass changes in educational policy and procedures, large class sizes, lack of resources, and poor relationships with administrators (Marston, Courtney, & Brunetti, 2006). Additionally, teacher job dissatisfaction is also a result of the lack of student motivation, lack of teacher influence over decision making, and student discipline problems (Ingersoll, 2001b). Job dissatisfaction leads to stress and to burnout if left unaddressed (Pearson & Moomaw, 2005).

Many teachers continue in their profession despite the obstacles confronted routinely. Public school teachers contend with challenging work conditions such as highly diverse student populations, deteriorating facilities, inadequate equipment and supplies, large class sizes, lack of respect from the public, changing expectations from administration and parents, and low salaries (Marston, Courtney, & Brunetti, spring 2006). Marston et al. (2006) determined that although elementary and middle school teachers differ in various ways, they are remarkably similar in their high degree of satisfaction with their jobs, and the devotion to "core professional values" motivates them to remain in the classroom. The level of career satisfaction has kept many teachers in the profession for 15 or more years (Marston, Courtney, & Brunetti, spring 2006).

Shann (1998) described teacher job satisfaction as a multifaceted construct that appears to be strongly related to teacher retention and school effectiveness. Teachers are most satisfied with teacher-pupil relationships (Marston, Courtney, & Brunetti, spring 2006). Ladson-Billings (1994) revealed that effective teachers place significant emphasis on student-teacher relationships. Parent-teacher relationships were the area of least satisfaction and greatest concern among the respondents (Marston, Courtney, & Brunetti, spring 2006). Kim and Loadman (1994) reported the following seven statistically significant predictors of job satisfaction: positive interactions with students and with colleagues, professional challenges, professional autonomy, tolerable working conditions, decent salary, and opportunities for advancement. Dinham (1994) divided sources of teacher satisfaction and dissatisfaction into the affective domain and school structure/administration with the greatest source of satisfaction in pupil achievement.

<u>Sexual Division of Labor</u>

In terms of men in general rejecting teaching as a profession, many do because they view it as a woman's profession. According to Thornton and Bricheno (2008), in most societies, work is gendered, and there is a division of labor along gender lines. Traditionally, men are employed as logging workers, automotive and body technicians, masons, bus and truck mechanics, electric power-line installers and repairers, tool and die makers, roofers, heavy equipment operators and service technicians, home appliance technicians, crane operators, doctors, business owners, bankers, and truck drivers. Women, on the other hand, are most often employed as nurses, dental hygienists, preschool and kindergarten teachers, secretaries and administrative assistants, dental assistants, speech-language pathologists, childcare workers, hairdressers/stylists, receptionists and information clerks, payroll and timekeeping clerks, and teacher assistants (Swift, 2007). Of course, there are many other occupations that we have not listed, but we can all agree that there are specific jobs associated with either one gender or the other, and teaching is no different. It is unfortunate that in an era in which the world has all but dissolved gender lines in the workplace in favor of competence and effectiveness, there are still people who attach a feminine stigma to the teaching profession, especially in the lower grades.

Dennis Wisemann (2004), in an article published on the Gender Public Advocacy Coalition's website entitled "Shortage of Male Teachers Worsens in Elementaries-Stereotypes Add to the Imbalance," says he went to college in the seventies to become an elementary school teacher, even though his friends dismissed it as women's work. Wisemann is in a school where female teachers outnumber male teachers 5 to 1. Some researchers say that gaps like these are widening. The National Education Association (NEA) (2004) reported that the percentage of male teachers had declined from 34 percent in 1971 to about 25 percent in 2003, even as gender stereotypes broke down in other occupations.

According to Bryan G. Nelson, author of "The Importance of Men Teachers: And Reasons why there are so Few," a Survey of Members of the National Association for the Education of Young Children:

> Understanding the factors that discourage men from teaching young children can help expand our knowledge about segregation of men's and women's

careers. It can also assist in addressing the problem of racism. Currently, there are few teachers that are men of color. Increasing the number of men of color in teaching will ensure better representation in classrooms matching the characteristics of the children in many of the communities served. Historically, challenging gender and race segregation has required changing attitudes and eliminating stereotypes that served as barriers for generations. It will require similar efforts to increase the number of men teachers; particularly, men of color. Fortunately, the Civil Rights and Women's Movement have provided the groundwork to challenge men's segregation from working with young children (2002).

In light of all of this negative press, why would anyone, let alone men, decide to enter the profession?

CHAPTER 2

Why Don't More Black Men Choose to go into Teaching?

According to Lewis (2005), "Jones [Stan Jones] believes there are many reasons why Black men choose to explore other careers like law, engineering, and healthcare. The first reason goes back to why men in general don't choose to become teachers, according to Jones. Teaching and some of the other fields mentioned in the previous section are often viewed as feminine."

Financial Stability

As Black men, ourselves, we (two of the three authors of the book) were not a part of this "gotta' make a million dollars" (or look like you make a million dollars) to have self-worth movement. We were a part of the "go to college, get a degree, get a 'good' job making an honest living" movement. It did not matter to our parents if we chose to go to college to be a social worker, a teacher, a probation officer, a lawyer, a doctor, a veterinarian, an accountant, or whatever. Our parents just knew that the chances of getting "good" jobs with benefits increased if we went to college. If we got good jobs with benefits, then we could each marry a young lady with a degree and a good job with benefits, and we could move into modest homes with white picket fences and have 2.5 kids and a dog. We could drive sedans, and our wives could drive minivans. How quaint.

Black boys (who, by the way, eventually grow up to be Black men) see Black professional athletes, Black singers, Black actors, and Black businessmen on television basking in the glow of wealth. These Black boys would certainly aspire to be more than mere "teachers." After all, teachers are not surrounded by beautiful, sexy women; teachers do not drive custom-built Maybachs and convertible Mercedes; they don't generally sail on luxury yachts and drink expensive liquors or even get invited to world premieres. They just "baby sit" other people's bad kids all day. (That's no fun, huh?) Teaching has also notoriously been known as a field in which the pay never meets the demands of the job" (Lewis 2005).

Why Do Black Men Leave the Profession?

In contrast to the Black men who choose not to enter the profession, there are dedicated Black men who choose to teach but are confronted with obstacles within the classroom that create a lack of desire to remain in the profession as a lifelong career. Historically, teachers require special support from educational leaders to ensure they become highly-qualified veteran teachers rather than casualties of teacher attrition (Quinn & Andrews, 2004). In our discourse with Black male educators, many of them discussed situations that occurred during their first two or three years of teaching that would have led to them to resign if it were not for knowledgeable, strong, and caring individuals who provided them with some kind of support. The support came in various forms, including lesson plans, a listening ear, advice about who to avoid and who to trust, a cautious warning when trouble was afoot, reminders about deadlines, advice about dealing with difficult parents. The support doesn't necessarily have to come from African Americans. People of different races who understand the challenges that come with being a young, Black man in education are invaluable resources, as well. The principal is one of the most important people in the lives of teachers (Brock & Grady, 1997). As a result, the principal is paramount to teachers' perceptions of feeling supported (Richards, 2004). According to Quinn and Andrews (2004), "Elementary, middle school, and high school principals have a powerful impact on the schools in their charge. The current teacher shortage combined with the demands of standards-based education place a strain on the teacher-principal relationship" (p.164).

Another factor that may contribute to the shortage of Black male teachers is that they frequently work within paradigms where they have the title, but no authority to employ change. For example, many Black male teachers work within the confines of controlling policymakers who strangle their ability to implement best practices for students (Quinn and Andrews, 2004). Most educators will attest to the fact that there are times when theory and practice do not agree. Because many educational theorists and policymakers have never graced the inside of a classroom in a public school, they do not truly understand what it takes to make things work. Sometimes, school divisions buy into these theories blindly, and there are educational leaders who cannot see past the theory to make changes based on a combination of research and experience. These shortsighted policymakers handcuff principals and other educational leaders to theories that do not hold water and do not fit the situation, the school, or the student.

CHAPTER 3

Why *Should* African American Men Choose Teaching as a Career?

I was escorting a visiting superintendent (who happened to be an African American male) on a visit to a kindergarten class in a suburban school division located in Virginia when a little Caucasian boy looked up at him and said, "It's Martin Luther King, Jr. raised from the dead." I said, "No, sweetie; this is a superintendent from . . ." I asked the student why he responded to our visitor the way he did, and he replied, "Because he is Black, and he is wearing a suit like Martin Luther King, Jr." I remember thinking to myself, "WOW! How many opportunities will he really get to see an African-American male educator or administrator between now and the time he graduates from high school?"

Diversity and Destruction of Stereotypes

African Americans, in general, should consider becoming teachers because they are vital to the future of a culturally diverse work force. African American teachers' limited presence negatively affects culturally isolated students who society does not provide with learning opportunities from teachers of different ethnic backgrounds. In terms of African American men, children of all races and nationalities need to see thorough, well-spoken, African American men in academic settings. The presence of such men can be the first step in dispelling the stereotypes associated with Black men.

We were reluctant to write this portion of the book because we assume everyone knows the stereotypes associated with Black men. In addition to that, neither of us is in the practice of spending our downtime mulling over and wallowing in the things that society says and believes about African American men, nor do we condone rehearsing the song "'bout how da' man tuk' us from Africa, dun' brung us ova' here, enslave usen, set us free, den' enslave us agin in da' money system." We elaborate on the stereotypes as a reminder for those who have forgotten and a lesson for those who are not cognizant of them. There is a need to include several other very important pieces of information before elaborating on the stereotypes.

1. We did not have to do research on this part from a book. (Our lives serve as the research.)
2. We all grew up in middle-class families with both of our parents, and we know that one does not have to grow up in an impoverished community to be affected by or associated with stereotypes.
3. We are not "right-wing" Blacks.
4. There are people (even Black men) who will deny that what we say is true, but there are countless other Black people and people of other nationalities who (if they are true to themselves) will substantiate the fact that stereotypes about Black men are a reality.
5. There are Black people who stereotype other Black people.

Okay, now that we have stated our disclaimers, here are some of the stereotypes associated with Black males:

- All Black men are violent.
- All Black men use slang and broken English.
- All Black men really love fried chicken and watermelon. (Maybe not together, but supposedly these are numbers one and two on our list of culinary delights.)
- All Black men can dance, and they love to sing and dance (perform) before a crowd.
- All Black men play sports well.

Some of these may sound ridiculous, but for those who would dispute our claim, we would ask you to think about the following: How many times has a Black man been asked to lead the "group" in song at work? Or how many times have the non-Black men at work invited the Black male(s) on the job to play basketball but left them out of the Poker game?

We would ask that those who deny the existence of such absurdities as stereotypes in post-modern America read and cogitate on the information in the following articles. The first is about a Black man who . . .

tries hard not to scare people. He is 6 foot 7, a garrulous lawyer who talks with his hands. And he's Black. Many people find him threatening. He works hard to prove otherwise. 'I have a very keen sense of my size and how I communicate,' says the Mason, Ohio resident. 'I end up putting my hands in my pockets or behind me. I stand with my feet closer together. With my feet spread out, it looks like I'm taking a stance. And I use a softer voice.'

Every day, African American men make a conscious effort to avoid personifying the stereotypes that epitomize them in the media, on television, and in movies. Some smile a lot, dress conservatively and speak with deference: "Yes, sir," or "No, ma'am." They're mindful of their bodies, careful not to dart into closing elevators or stand too close in grocery stores. It's all about surviving and trying to thrive in a nation where biased views of Black men stubbornly hang on decades after segregation and where statistics show a yawning gap between the lives of White men and Black men. Black men's median wages are barely three-fourths those of Whites. Nearly 1 in 3 Black men will spend time behind bars during his lifetime, and on average, Black men die six years earlier than White men (Textiera, 2006).

Sure, everyone has ways of coping with the way they think (or know) they are perceived by other people. Which professionals act the same at work as they do with their children or their friends? But for Black men, there's more at stake. If they don't carefully calculate how to handle everyday situations (in ways that usually go unnoticed), they can end up out of a job, in jail, or dead. Learning to adapt is at the heart of being an American Black male. 'Black mothers and fathers socialize their sons not to make waves, to not come up against the authorities, to speak even more politely not only when Whites are present, but particularly if there are Whites who have power'" (Textiera, 2006). These parents teach their children to do this as a part of the "game," not because a feeling or sense of inferiority.

In the second of four segments of the article by Textiera related to stereotypes, a 43 year old business owner from New Orleans compares stereotype avoidance to a game of chess. He says that he has even taught his three sons, ages 16, 14, and 11 to play the game. "Most Black men are able to shift from a sort of relaxed, authentically Black pose into a respectable Black man pose." At times, the style of clothes that Black men wear can serve as the catalyst for stereotyping. Another article makes reference to a twenty year old African American male from Brooklyn who is well aware that wearing baggy jeans and an over-sized t-shirt makes him seem like "another one of those thuggish Black kids." The antithesis of his "thugged out" look is what he calls his "Southern Charm." This "Southern Charm" includes lots of "Yes ma'ams" and very little slang. This strategy (according to the man mentioned in the article) causes Whites to perceive him differently (in a positive way). This young man, like other African Americans, knows that these "skillful changes" in style, speech, and mannerisms are not spoken of widely outside of Black circles. It goes far beyond code switching. "Historians agree that Black stereotypes and coping strategies are rooted in America's history of slavery and segregation" (2006).

We are *not* saying that Black men should walk around and be hypersensitive when it comes to stereotypes. Black men are not the only people who are stereotyped, and stereotypes will always be a part of the world's culture because people will always speculate about what they do not know or do not understand. We *are* saying that having a thorough, articulate, African American male teacher in the classroom can do wonders for dispelling these stereotypes for Black children and children of other races. This teacher will not change people's opinions based on what he says; he will change people's minds based on who he is.

Change Perceptions of Black Men as Leaders

Having thorough Black men in the classroom and in leadership positions in education can also give people more confidence in the power of Black men to lead. This is critical because school-aged children formulate opinions about people and things that they carry over into adulthood. Chmelynshi (2006) affirms, "All students need to see Black males in authority roles—roles of responsibility, academic roles showing there are manifestations of Black maleness other than athletics, entertainment, or, unfortunately, crime" (p. 42). The things they see, hear, and experience during their formative years have a significant impact on them. Imagine how amazing it would be if children of different nationalities were exposed to thorough, articulate, African American males as teachers! It would be even more amazing if those thorough, articulate, African American teachers developed meaningful, productive relationships with the families of their students. Imagine members of Asian, Latino, Russian, and/or Caucasian families sitting around the dinner table sharing school and childhood stories that included positive stories about teachers. Imagine if some of these positive teachers were Black . . . men.

Our parents always taught us that "You never get a second chance to make a first impression." Unfortunately, many individuals base their perceptions of people they have just met or strangers with whom they come in contact on television or literary archetypes. Archetypal characters or stock characters are the original patterns or models from which all things of the same kind are copied or on which they are based. Some of the most popular archetypes are: the absent-minded professor, the ditzy blonde, the crusader, the hen-pecked husband, the dumb jock, the nerd, and the hero. Unfortunately, these images seep into our minds, and it is difficult for some people to separate fiction from reality. As a result, people like jocks and blondes who visibly fit particular archetypes have to work tirelessly to prove that they are different.

As most of us watched the 2008 presidential race, it was apparent that (now) President Barack Obama's ideas were not the major focus of the first part of the campaign; his competence and integrity were in question because for some people, it is rare to see an

African American male who is the proverbial "total package." Maybe, just maybe, if seeing thorough, articulate, Black men was the norm in our country, people could have focused on his political platform first because it would not have been such an anomaly to see a Black man in a leadership role. This norm can begin in America's classrooms with thorough, articulate, Black men because each time Black people see a thorough, articulate, intelligent Black man, it gives them hope that there are more of them around. Conversely, each time people see an unpolished, unrefined thug, or a "pseudo-polished," wanna-be refined, quasi-articulate imposter, their stereotypes about Black men are confirmed.

Take a moment to cogitate on the following scenarios and their possible impact on the perception of Black men.

Beth

Beth is an eleventh grader at a predominately White public school. She comes from an upper middle class family. Her church is all White; her brother's soccer team is all White; her dance class is all White (except for that one Black girl named Janice who is not really like a Black girl because she tucks her course hair behind her ear, and she does that hair toss like the White girls, and she also talks like all of Beth's other friends, and her family is one of two Black families that live in Beth's neighborhood); her mother's friends are all White; her dad's friends are all White; only White people come to her parents' holiday parties; all of the people she idolizes are White; and all of her teachers have been White (and she goes to public school . . . go figure). Beth's family is not prejudiced, nor do they harbor any ill-will towards Black people. They see Black people at the community grocery store, the mall, restaurants, and other places. The secretary at her dad's office is a really nice Black lady who her family adores.

What Black men does she see? Well, she sees a few Black rappers on MTV. They are thugs who love money, sex, cars, jewelry, and fame. They perform in the midst of scantily clad Black women shakin' that thang, making their booties clap, droppin' it like it's hot, and twerking for all of the ballers and bosses. These girls may also be in a limousine waiting for their chance to "lick the (w)rapper." Beth's parents (like most parents) don't really like for her to watch that stuff. She may see a Black male athlete or two on television. The other Black man she may see on television (during Black History Month) is Reverend

Dr. Martin Luther King, Jr. Beth may even see a Black news reporter on television from time to time. The African American male she sees in person on a regular basis is the custodian at her school. Oh, and Janice's dad when he picks her up from dance class and attends recitals. There are a whole lot of Black men outside of these, men like Janice's dad who have college degrees and work as salesmen, computer programmers, pastors, engineers, attorneys, accountants, hotel and restaurant managers, real estate agents, supervisors, writers, and yes, educators. There are also other good Black men who are entrepreneurs, mechanics, truck drivers, carpenters, brick layers, etc.

Right now, we suspect that the value Beth places on African American males is pretty low if they are not on television. What would happen if Beth had a thorough, masculine, articulate, and caring African American male as a teacher? (We only mention masculine because sometimes people do not put thorough and masculine together when it comes to African American men in the classroom. The masculine teacher is placed in the category with the stereotypical jock.) **What would Beth see? How would this affect her in the long run?**

- It might help put the notion that all Black men are violent to rest.
- It may also put the notion that all Black men speak using "Ebonics" to rest.
- It may give her a more positive perception of other Black men with whom she comes in contact.
- Maybe (just maybe) the next time she hears someone make a categorical statement like "all Black men are . . ." she will be able to confidently stand up and say: "Not **all** Black men are that way."
- Beth may also realize that Black men can have a productive relationship with students without wanting anything from them other than their academic best.

Keshia J.

Keshia J. is an African American female from the inner city. She is in the ninth grade, and she attends a school that is predominately Black. Her mother has six children by five different men, none of whom bothered to stay around or pay child support. Keshia's mother is on welfare, and the family lives with her aunt in a housing project. She also has two uncles who live in the house as well. One is twenty, and the other is eighteen. Neither of them graduated from high school; neither is employed. They jump from one job to the next, never keeping a job for more than two months. Once they quit or lose a job, they stay unemployed for six months and "mooch" off of her mother and her grandmother. Each has been in and out of jail several times. Their excuse for everything deals with "the man." The younger uncle has a two-year old, and the older uncle has a baby on the way. Keshia has only seen her father two times in her life. Now he is locked up for larceny. She does not know her grandfather, because her grandmother was a single parent.

Keshia is physically mature for her age. She is always receiving compliments and propositions from young boys, as well as older men. Every time she turns around, someone is talking to her about *her* body and *their* intentions. She was even offered a car one time. There was another time when one of her mother's boyfriends came over when her mother was not at home. The boyfriend propositioned her and even began forcing himself on her until he heard one of her siblings coming in from school. Her mother read that sucker the riot act and dismissed him after that. This one takes the cake! One time, she could have sworn that the preacher at her grandmother's church was looking at her with lustful intentions (but she could not be sure of that, after all, he is a preacher).

Keshia watches BET and MTV. She sees the way the guys live and all of the bling they flash. She sees the girls in the videos and hears the guys call the girls "bitches" and "whores," but she knows they are not talking about all girls. They are just talking about the groupies. She hears all the rappers talk about sex, and she watches the girls in the videos respond to them. (This sets her up to have very unhealthy and destructive relationships with men, unbeknownst to her.)

What would happen if Keshia had a thorough, masculine, articulate, and caring Black man as a teacher? **What would Keshia glean from this experience? How would this affect her in the long run?** Maybe having a teacher like this will give her hope.

- She might see that there are other men like her teacher, who see the value in her mind . . . not her body.
- She might see that Black men *can* hold down a job and be stable.
- Maybe Keshia would have one man who she could respect and honor. Maybe this would

lead to her respecting other Black men, and sowing positive seeds into the Black men around her.

- Maybe Keshia would learn to communicate with Black men about topics other than sex, drugs, babies, drama, and other frivolous things.

- Keshia might be able to envision a model for a husband. After all, there are many women who marry men who are like their fathers.

- If the teacher is married and has a strong family, she might learn something about families and positive relationships between husbands and wives.

The possibilities are endless.

Carlos

Carlos is a fourteen year old boy from California. He is a member of a gang. Carlos actually liked school a lot, but he was ridiculed by the other boys in the neighborhood. They called him a "school boy;" they waited for him at the corner and chased him home or beat him up. His parents dismissed it as "boy stuff," but this was serious. He dropped out of school and joined the gang when he got to the ninth grade. He saw this as the only alternative. During his initiation, he had to fight two members of the gang at the same time. He came away with a bloody nose, some bruised ribs, and a swollen eye, but he was finally in. Deep in his heart, he hoped that his father would see his bruises and decide to move somewhere else where he could go to school, but his father didn't pay any attention and did not allow his mother to pay attention either. As a matter of fact, he heard his father tell his mother that the fight might toughen him up a little. At that point, Carlos gave up any hope of ever going back to school. When they were out of school, the other members of the gang talked about how awful school was, how they felt like they were in jail when they were there, and how much of a waste of time it was because only the rich "school boys" got the breaks. The only time they went around school now was to recruit new gang members or to socialize with the girls. They would hang around for an hour or so during lunch, then the police would come and chase them away. Carlos knew that most of the teachers were glad that kids like these were not in school. Most of the teachers were scared of them, and they were such behavior problems in class that days without them were much more peaceful and productive. Carlos never acted up in class when he was there because he wanted to do something different than the people around him. He wanted to be a teacher himself so he could help other kids like him. He saw the way that some of the teachers looked at him and the other Latinos. Some of the teachers pitied them, so they passed them along from one grade to the next (even if they had not learned anything). Others gave the rough boys candy to pacify them while they were in classroom and passed them because they were afraid of them. Some of the female teachers had a genuine interest, but they could only go so far without being ridiculed by their co-workers (especially since the scandal involving the female teacher and the Latino boy.) Carlos . . . a lost cause.

What might happen if Carlos and the other members of the gang had a strong, caring, minority, male teacher? Someone who understands the plight of the minority man . . .

- Maybe Carlos would see that minority men can be successful.
- Maybe he would see some hope for himself and other boys like him.

When people think of Black men in the classroom, they usually think of role models for Black boys. The truth is that a thorough, caring, nurturing teacher can make positive changes in the world and in people's mindsets regardless of race or gender, but there must also be balance. There is no balance in education because the voice of the Black man and his contribution to the collective intelligence of Americans is missing.

Veleka S. Gatling, Ph.D.

I had an African American male role model as a classroom teacher. My sixth grade teacher stood six feet tall. His demeanor commanded the attention of even the most obstinate students. In contrast to the female teachers I had, he did not raise his voice to get the class' attention when we were unusually loud; he lowered his voice. He understood how important it was to project a different image of Blacks to all of us. He especially knew how important it was for my classmates who did not have a positive male role model in the form of a father, grandfather, uncle, etc. present in the home. Some of the students in my class tried to "test" him from time to time, but his demeanor was consistent, even when they misbehaved. When members of my class would misbehave, he would say, 'I love you, but I don't like your behavior.' When there was strife among members of the class, he would say: "This class is your family, and we will respect each other. You don't have to like each other, but you do have to respect each other." One day, several of my classmates were goofing off during the Pledge of Allegiance. Mr. Smith did not fuss at us. He made us look up the words we did not know the meaning of in the Pledge of Allegiance then he taught a lesson on what the Pledge of Allegiance meant to us as Americans and why we should be respectful.

Mr. Smith was the quintessential educator because he played many roles and taught lessons that transcended the classroom. He provided security/ protection for me and the other children in the class who were the teased for various reasons. He didn't allow my classmates to joke me because I wore special shoes to help straighten the curve in my spine. He taught us vital lessons about penmanship. He would always say, "You need good penmanship until you become famous. Then you can write any way you want." His handwriting was among the neatest I had ever seen, and he encouraged all of us to perfect our penmanship.

My father was certainly a sufficient role model at home. In addition to my father, my grandfather, my uncles, and other male family members painted a comprehensive picture of the role that men should play in the life of a young girl. Having a teacher like Mr. Smith was extra special to me because I saw many of the same positive qualities in my father, my grandfather, my uncles, and other male family members. Mr. Smith confirmed what I knew manhood to be (from a young lady's perspective). I still keep in touch with Mr. Smith. Each year, I call to wish him happy birthday (we share the same birth month). When I graduated from high school, I invited him and several other teachers to my parents' home for my graduation party.

Cultural Sensitivity and Empathy

"There is a greater chance for academic demise among students whose cultural characteristics are devalued or unrecognized" (King, 1993). "Many teachers of color have valuable insight into the cultures of their students. Based on their experiences, this particular group of teachers is often well versed in the sociocultural realities faced by many students in these communities, and they can use this information to inform their practice" (Irizarry, 2007).

Non-Black teachers need teachers of color in order to gain an understanding of effective ways to communicate and deal with students of color in some cases. ÒLee, Lomotey and Shujaa (1990) contend that an African American teaching perspective is needed to produce an education that contributes to achieving pride, equity, power, wealth, and cultural continuity (p. 47), as well as to advance character development within the context of the African American community and culture (King, 1993, p. 117).

There are people and events that are important to Black people that teachers of other cultures don't necessarily recognize or understand. Without this understanding, the examples that these non-Black teachers use as they teach do not carry as much meaning for African American students. Some of these events are the Million Man March, the Los Angeles Riot, the O.J. Simpson trial and verdict, the election of Barack Obama as the first Black President of the United States of America, the Gena 6 saga, the Trayvon Martin murder case, the murder of Biggie Smalls and Tupac Shakur. A few of these important people are President Barack Obama, First Lady Michelle Obama, Nas, Oprah Winfrey, Dr. Jawanza Kunjufu, Terry McMillan, Public Enemy, Tom Joyner, Tyler Perry, Kirk Franklin, Denzel Washington, Reverend Al Sharpton, Reverend Jesse Jackson, and Bishop T.D. Jakes.

In terms of cultural sensitivity, it is not the writers' assertion that Black men have the answers for all Black boys and Black children in general. It *is* our assertion that Black men understand the dynamics of the world from a Black perspective. It *is* our assertion that teachers of other races and nationalities cannot teach Black boys how to navigate life from a Black perspective. The manner in which Black men have to navigate the world in search of success and acceptance is different because the world views them differently, and it is the responsibility of other Black men (and women) to teach them how. Here are a few examples:

1. Black men have to wear a suit in order to be considered dressed up, but other men can wear khakis, loafers, and a polo shirt. African

American boys need to know this so they show up for a job interview dressed to impress.

2. The manner in which African Americans speak is important when it comes to success in the workplace and promotion. People expect broken English and slang when African Americans speak, especially in the South. Proficient use of the English language is imperative if Black boys (who grow up to be Black men) are to be taken seriously in the workplace.

3. The manner in which African Americans write is another factor that determines the potential for advancement in many career fields.

4. African American males have to be very strategic about workplace associations.

CHAPTER 4

Role Models

Can Black Men Be Role Models for Boys of Other Races?

Years ago, when Charles Barkley was in the NBA, he made a point of saying that he was not a role model. He wanted to do what he wanted, say what he wanted, and compete the way he wanted without any moral recourse. The truth is that he could not help being a role model. He, like Michael Jordan, Scotty Pippen, Mark Price, Kevin McHale and the rest of his contemporaries in the NBA, was a role model whether he liked it or not. The White athletes were not just role models for the White children, nor were the Black athletes just role models for the Black children. Those athletes were role models for children who wanted to be great.

Back in the 70's and 80's when Larry Bird was one of the premier players in the NBA, it was not unusual to hear young Black boys on the playground say that they wanted to pass the ball or shoot like Larry Bird. It did not matter that Larry Bird was White. What mattered was that the Celtics could count on him when they needed him. He always came through. Of course, there were boys who wanted to pass the ball like Magic Johnson on NBA "dream courts" across America, but when our friends mentioned Larry Bird, no one stopped the game and said: "You can't be like Larry Bird; he's White and you're Black." It didn't matter. The only thing that mattered was that he was good.

When we played football in the back yard, there were boys who wanted to run the ball like John Riggins, a White fullback who played for the Washington Redskins. There were those who wanted to throw the ball like Miami's Bob Griese and Dallas' Roger Staubach (both White quarterbacks). Our friends who aspired to run the ball like Riggins and throw the ball like Griese and Stabach knew that there were Black running backs like Tony Dorsett of the Dallas Cowboys and Walter Payton of the Chicago Bears, but they wanted to run the ball like John Riggins. One of the most fabulous catches in a championship game was made by Gary Clark of the San Francisco 49ers, and we all had friends who saw that and wanted to catch like Gary Clark. Did it matter that Clark, or Greise, or Staubach, or Riggins were White? No!

During the summers (literally the summer time) of our youth, many of us had the unfortunate "privilege" of watching soap operas on rainy days when we were "trapped" in the house. There was a character on "The Young and the Restless" named Victor Newman. Victor was a sober-minded, intelligent businessman. He was handsome; he had class, style, and savior-faire. He was also well-spoken, eclectic, and fearless. Victor was the quintessential sex symbol. Women loved him, men envied him, and at least one Black boy wanted to be like him. Of course, lots of young men wanted to be like Billy D. Williams, Denzel Washington, and "Ponch" (Eric Estrada) from CHIPs, too. It did not matter that Ponch and Victor were not Black. The point we are laboriously trying to make is that it should not make a difference what color a person is. Personality traits do not have color. If a person is cool, he or she is just friggin' cool; if a person is smart, he or she is just smart; if a person is good looking, he or she is just good looking. The same goes for sex appeal, brilliance, savior-faire, fastidiousness, artistic talent, etc. People who have the X Factor just have the X Factor. This begs the question: "Can Black men be role models for boys of other races?" The resounding answer is "Yes!"

Let's look at some African American icons from the past and present whose influence has crossed and still crosses color lines. These Black men have set the standard for people in general (not just African Americans) because of their resolve, work ethic, commitment to education, commitment to erudition, and unending pursuit of civil rights and equality.

President Barack Obama

The most obvious Black man whose influence crosses color lines is the 44th President of the United States of America, Barack Obama. First and foremost, the world was amazed by Barack the man. This Black man was articulate, intelligent, savvy, confident, and refined. When he began his campaign, most Americans did not know who he was; some did not care to get to know him because they didn't want to be disappointed by the same things that disappoint us in so many other Black "leaders": inarticulate speech, a dearth of elegance, and a consistently tumultuous personal life. As a matter of fact, there were lots of people who did not take a second look at (then) Senator Barack Obama until the battle between he and Hillary Clinton for the Democratic nomination escalated. The more people watched him, the more impressed they were, and his approval ratings showed that an overwhelming majority of Americans shared this sentiment. As the presidential campaign progressed, people got an opportunity to see the many faces of Barack Obama. America had an opportunity to observe his response to pressure, ridicule, praise, cynicism, racism, and the other stimuli to which all political candidates are subject. One of the most memorable moments in the campaign occurred during the second debate. Senator John McCain referred to Senator Barack Obama as "that one" during one of his rebuttals. Most people would have reacted, but (then) Senator Obama was stoic. That one reaction or "non-reaction" solidified Barack Obama as the choice for many Americans who were undecided. Even the most skeptical voters could not deny the fact that a man who had worked and lived honorably enough to earn respect had just been publicly and personally disrespected, yet he remained unflustered. This man had what it took to be America's next President.

In addition to being worthy of emulation as an individual, President Obama has proven himself to be worthy of respect as a family man. We *are no*t saying that the Obama's have a perfect marriage or a perfect family; we *are* saying that the values that they are teaching their children and the methods that he and his wife use to solve problems must be working. He has proven to be worthy of the emulation of young men and old men of all races. Barack Obama does not bear this distinction alone. There are other Black men who have proven to be worthy of admiration from people of other races.

We are well aware that this is not a book about the achievements of African American men, but we would be remiss if we did not mention a few other African American men who are worthy of emulation from men and boys of all races.

Michael Jordan

Michael Jordan is another Black man whose influence crosses color lines. Michael Jordan was one of the greatest basketball players and athletes to ever set foot on the court. One of the most amazing stories surrounding Michael Jordan involves him being cut from his high school basketball team his sophomore year. Jordan wasn't willing to accept defeat; he worked tirelessly on his game and tried out for the team again the following year. Jordan made the team the next two years, received a scholarship to the University of North Carolina at Chapel Hill, and the rest is history. Here is what Hubie Brown, sports analyst and former NBA head coach, had to say about Jordan's career. According to Brown (2001), "Looking back at Michael Jordan's long and illustrious career, I think the quality that sets him apart from all other players is that he set the bar of excellence at such a high level that in our immediate future, his status is unlikely to ever be challenged."

Michael Jordan is not just known for his accomplishments on the basketball court; he is also known for his copious product endorsements. He has done endorsements for Coca Cola, Gatorade, Nike, Wilson, Haynes, McDonalds, Chevrolet, MCI, Rayovac, Wheaties, and many other companies (Vancil, 1991). In addition to endorsing several high-profile products, Jordan has starred and appeared in several movies. Jordan is a philanthropist, an entrepreneur, a father, and an avid golfer. Michael Jordan is also on the list of Black men who are worthy to be emulated by young men of all races because he is refined and articulate.

Benjamin Carson, M.D.

Yet another Black man who has made an indelible mark in history is Dr. Benjamin Carson. Dr. Carson was born in Detroit, Michigan. He was one of two children in a poor, single-family household. Although his mother only had a third-grade education, she challenged him to strive for excellence. Carson struggled early in his academic career, but he eventually rose from the bottom to the top of his class. His achievements earned him academic scholarships to college and medical school. Dr. Carson went on to become the Director of Pediatric Neurosurgery at Johns Hopkins Hospital at age 33. He is world-renowned for leading a medical team that separated West German conjoined twins in 1987, as well as leading a team of South African doctors in the first successful separation of vertically conjoined twins in 1997 ("Ben Carson Biography," 2013).

Russell Simmons

Russell Simmons is a visionary of rap, record producer, manager, (former) co-owner and founder of the rap label Def Jam Records and head of Rush Artist Management. An ambitious entrepreneur, Russell Simmons viewed Def Jam as just a part of his hip hop empire. His firm, Rush Communications, also included Phat Farm clothing company, television shows, a management company, a magazine, and an advertising agency. His movie production company has produced such films as *Krush Groove* and *The Nutty Professor,* starring Eddie Murphy. In 1999, he sold his stake in Def Jam Records to Universal Music Group for $100 million. In 2004, he sold Phat Farm for $140 million.

Simmons is also an active philanthropist. He is one of the founders of the Hip Hop Summit Action Network, the Rush Philanthropic Organization, and the Foundation for Ethnic Understanding. Simmons is an active PETA supporter and was named a Goodwill Ambassador to fight war, poverty, and HIV/AIDS. He is the author of *Do You!: 12 Laws to Access the Power in You to Achieve Happiness and Success* ("Russell Simmons biography," 2013).

The Honorable L. Douglas Wilder

L. Douglas Wilder graduated from Virginia Union University in Richmond, VA with a degree in chemistry. He is a decorated veteran of the Korean War, and he was awarded the Bronze Star for heroism in combat. After the war, he returned to Richmond and worked as a chemist in the state medical examiner's office. He studied law at Howard University in Washington, D.C. He received his degree in 1959, and after passing the Bar in Virginia, established his own law firm, Wilder, Gregory, and Associates.

In 1969, Wilder entered politics, running in a special election for the Virginia State Senate. He won and became the first African American state senator in Virginia since The Reconstruction. Wilder spent ten years in the General Assembly and was recognized as one of its most effective legislators. Wilder was elected lieutenant governor in 1985. Four years later, he ran for statewide office again, and on January 13, 1990, L. Douglas Wilder became Virginia's sixty-sixth governor. He was the first elected African American governor in United States history. During his administration, Wilder was lauded for his sound fiscal management and his ability to balance the state budget during difficult economic times. He sponsored new construction projects at many of Virginia's colleges and universities, mental health facilities, and state parks. After promoting the idea of a popularly elected mayor for Richmond, Wilder was overwhelmingly elected to the post in November 2004 (Kelly & Dozier, 2010).

Andrew Young

Andrew Young received his B.S. in biology from Howard University when he was only 19 years old. Shortly thereafter, he enrolled in Hartford Theological Seminary where he received a bachelor of divinity and was ordained a minister in the United Church of Christ. He felt the call to do more than minister, though, and he began to answer the call to civil rights. He marched on the front lines with Dr. Martin Luther King, Jr. and was at the Lorraine Motel with Dr. King on the day that he was assassinated. Andrew Young was the first African American from Georgia to serve in the U.S. House of Representatives since the Reconstruction period. He returned to Congress in 1974 and 1976. President Jimmy Carter nominated Young as ambassador to the United Nations, and he was unanimously confirmed in 1977. Andrew Young also served two very successful terms as mayor of Atlanta and served as co-chair for the Atlanta Committee for the 1996 Olympic Games (New Georgia Encyclopedia: Andrew Young (b. 1932), n.d.).

Cornel West, Ph.D.

Dr. Cornel West is an American philosopher, scholar of African American studies, and political activist. His most influential book, *Race Matters* (1993), lamented what he saw as the spiritual impoverishment of the African American underclass and critically examined the "crisis of Black leadership" in America. In 1970, West (then 17 years old) entered Harvard University on scholarship. He graduated magna cum laude three years later with a bachelor's degree in Middle Eastern languages and literature. He attended graduate school at Princeton University, where he was influenced by the American pragmatist philosopher, Richard Rorty. After receiving his doctoral degree in 1980, West taught philosophy, religion, and African American studies at several colleges and universities, including Union Theological Seminary, Yale University (including the Yale Divinity School), the University of Paris, Princeton University, and Harvard University, where he was appointed

Alphonse Fletcher, Jr., University Professor in 1998. He returned to Princeton in 2002.

His best-known work, *Race Matters*, is a collection of essays which was published exactly one year after the start of riots in Los Angeles. These riots were directly related to the acquittal of four White police officers who brutalized an African American motorist by the name of Rodney King. The book discussed the pervasive despair and "nihilism" (The belief that all established authority is corrupt and must be destroyed in order to rebuild a just society.) of African Americans in poverty and criticized African American leaders for pursuing strategies that West believed were shortsighted, narrow-minded, or self-serving ("Cornel West biography," 2013).

This chapter highlights a few examples of Black men who have lived and worked in such a manner that they are worthy of emulation by people of all races. Excellence should not be determined by color. Erudition should not be tainted with racial and cultural epithets. Excellence and erudition are worthy of emulation by all; the race of the vessel (person) is of little consequence. When the question "Can an African American male be a role model for children of other races?" is posed, the answer is a resounding "Yes!"

CHAPTER 5

The Contemporary Black Teacher as a Role Model for Black Boys

We have explored the positive effects that thorough Black male teachers may have on students of other races and genders. The next question is: How would Black boys benefit from having a thorough, articulate, Black man as a teacher? It is no secret that many African American males experience various educational barriers that impede their ability to succeed. Specifically, African American male students often experience higher levels of substance abuse, violence, homelessness, imprisonment, unemployment, homicides, poor health, notably shorter life expectancy, and premature death (Cones & White, 1999; Chideya, 1999; Hutchison, 1995; Staples, 1989). The presence of positive, African American male teachers can help African American students navigate their academic environment, nurture their quest for knowledge, and provide the underpinnings that promote and encourage student excellence. Black male presence is also essential for the success of Black boys in school settings because the positive relationships they can forge are critical for building character and self-esteem.

For years, the whole "role model" idea was cliché. It seemed like every time we turned around, someone was talking about a role model. We were inundated with the phrase "role model" so much that some of us became physically ill and ill-tempered each time the phrase was uttered, written, implied, or at the formation of the phrase on someone's lips. Although the phrase has been overused, and the concept has been perverted in many cases, there is considerable merit in the role model concept. According to Erik Erikson's psychosocial theory of development, appropriate role models are necessary for students, particularly during adolescence (Powell 1983; Comer and Poussaint 1992). It may be more difficult for those of us who grew up with supportive fathers or grandfathers in the home to understand that people (not just children) need role models, but they do. We know the story of Black boys and role models, or the lack thereof. It is an age-old tale. In some cases, Black boys grow up in households that are devoid of accessible male role models. So what do they do? They watch the rappers and singers on television and mimic what they do. The fact that young Black boys can dress like these celebrities, rap and sing their songs, and (in some cases) relate to their experiences make rappers and singers more tangible, even if these impressionable, young boys never have the pleasure of meeting their idols. In time, these young men seek to emulate the rapper's life, or they endeavor to live the life that the rappers and singers sing and rap about. It takes consistent mentoring and teaching to keep some young men from ruining their lives chasing the fast life that is portrayed in some of our Rap and R & B music. That being said, African American male teachers and role models play a crucial role in helping African American boys to form their identities, identities that are grounded in reality and suited to their own, individual skill set. We *are not* saying that Black boys should not dream and seek to become what they dream. We *are* saying that African American male teachers can better assist these young men with a pathway to success and critical career counseling based on their skill set, especially those young men who are seeking careers in the entertainment industry.

In nuclear families, the father has the task of framing the structure that will support the rest of his son's personality traits. Fathers frame that structure with things like reverence for God, respect for one's mother, sister or sisters, and other women, respect for one's fellow man, respect for self, integrity, manly contemplativeness, and manly courage. Fathers also have the responsibility of teaching manly responses to things in life through the way they live. Oftentimes, dads need to explain why they respond to things the way they do, but that is all a part of raising a child. The father's responsibilities in the household as they relate to raising a son in no way diminish the role of the mother. There are single women who have raised sons who have achieved phenomenal success, but to say that it is not essential to have fathers in the home absolves all men from the responsibility, and that is not the way it is meant to be.

Each person is like a mosaic or a collage. No two people are exactly alike. There may be a profusion of similarities in certain individuals, but (again) no two people are just alike. A person forms his or her personality based on the influences around him or her that facilitate survival, result in acceptance from other people, and project an image for others to see. Outside stimuli provide a "buffet" from which a person can select to enhance to his or her personality. The point is that all boys need the same opportunity to create the mosaic or the collage that comprises his personality, and part of that mosaic should be formed based on successful men of one's own race who are "real people" as opposed to people on television or in the movies. There is a shortage of Black men from whom Black boys can glean positive attributes to add to their personalities and help shape their identities. Black male teachers can fill that void. Students get to see and "re-see" teachers 180+ days a year in all sorts of different situations. The word "respect" is comprised of the prefix "re," which means "again," and the root, "spect," which means "to see." When a person meets you for the first time, he or she can only "see" you, and most people will form some sort of opinion about who you are based on their experience with and knowledge of one who is "like" you. After they have known you for a while, they have an opportunity to take a second look at you. They can compare their initial impression of you with the "you" they know more intimately. In other words, they can truly "re-see" or re-spect you. In the case of African American male teachers and African American boys, the teacher has time to establish a relationship with these students, earn their trust, and earn their respect; then, and only then, should the student consider adding a component of that teacher's personality to his mosaic or collage without reservation.

For the Black boys who have a positive role model in their lives, the teacher may just confirm what these students already know about what it means to be a responsible man. If we were to examine the archetypal hero, we would find that there are things that make them different, but we would also find a set of values that they share that make them very similar. Dirty Harry, Shaft, Captain Luke Piccard, Spencer, McGiver, Batman, Superman, and Spiderman have lots of things that make them unique, but their core values are analogous. Such is the case with teachers, fathers, grandfathers, uncles, and other men who may be active in a boy's life. They may look very different on the outside; they may like different things, have different hobbies, or have different beliefs, but a male student can connect or identify with the core values that his teacher shares with his father, grandfather, stepfather, uncle, or another positive male role model; thus, confirming what he understands manhood to be and maybe adding some components to his definition of manhood.

Another way that black male teachers can make a difference in the lives of Black boys involves culturally responsive instruction. In his book: *Closing the Racial Academic Achievement Gap*, Matthew Lynch deals with the importance of "Culturally Responsive Instruction." According to Lynch & Carr (2006), In order to be successful, ". . . educators must understand the cultures of all students, including African Americans. The concept of culture affects the way students act, speak, dress, and behave. It is becoming more and more important that teachers create a classroom environment that welcomes individual differences and rejects stereotypes." Black men who teach other young Black men understand certain things about them because they have been in similar situations and experienced similar things. A Black male teacher may understand what it feels like to:

- have people laugh and scoff when you open up and share things like your educational and career plans and maybe your dreams about family,
- have people ignore your ideas in a group discussion or project,

- have people look at you funny when you answer a question *correctly* in class,
- have people hear your idea and reject it, but hear the same idea from a person of a different race and/or gender and think it is wonderful.

Teachers from other cultures should not use their own cultural background as a reference for how African Americans should behave or see the world. Educators must realize that it is no longer acceptable to use just one method of instruction for all students. Teachers need adequate, in-depth understanding of their students' backgrounds in order to select and incorporate culture-specific examples and material into the curriculum. This will accomplish two goals: It will make the material more relevant for students, and it will demonstrate the value that teacher has placed on understanding the background of his or her students (Lynch & Carr, 2006).

Black male teachers have the ability to relate to the issues facing Black students and assist majority teachers with best approaches for dealing with Black male students (Lewis, 2002). Every student doesn't need a teacher from his or her own culture in order to be successful, but it is critical for the majority of students to have a teacher who relates to them in some way. And there *should* be a proportionate number of teachers of a student's race along his or her educational path to assist them in understanding the ramifications of certain historical events and current events as these events relate to their race. African American males have been bereft of this for a number of years. Cogitate on this . . . How many years do Black boys go without a teacher who can identify with them? Is that the reason why so many Black boys drop out of school and never learn to value real education? Is the proportion of children who succeed in school and the extent to which they succeed related to the number of teachers they have who are of the same race and/or gender? According to Jacqueline Irvine, "cultural differences are often the source of disagreements between African American students and their teachers. If teachers are unaware of the cultural differences, they may view students' behavior negatively (Lynch & Carr 2006, p. 47). Even the African American female, as much as she can nurture and discipline her students from a maternal perspective, cannot completely understand the struggle that Black boys face. Undoubtedly, there are some behaviors that are wrong, regardless of race, but there are some behaviors that are perceived as threatening by teachers who are *not* African American men that would not be perceived that way by teachers who *are* African American men. African American male teachers can help teachers who are not African American understand the difference between an active boy and a boy who has a behavioral disorder.

According to Dr. Jawanza Kunjufu, 83% of all elementary teachers are female. Black children constitute 17% of all students and startlingly, 41% of all special education placements. Dr. Kunjufu takes an in-depth look at this issue. Parents, administrators, and educators should consider why Black children are disproportionately labeled with specific learning disabilities and emotionally disabilities. We should also pose the following questions: Why are Black boys placed in special education classes more than Black girls? Is there any relationship between female teachers and the disproportionate number of Black boys being found eligible for special education services and/or suspended? (Kunjufu, 2005). It is our assertion that thorough, articulate, African American male teachers can assist parents, other teachers, counselors, and administrators in determining the difference between bad behavior that can be offset with counseling versus an actual disability.

African American male teachers can also step into the students' world and make meaning out of chaos. There was an earlier reference to rap and hip-hop music and its' influence on young Black men in America. Our young men see the money, the women, the cars, the clubs, and the parties, and they think real life is that way for rappers and other artists. The problem, in many cases, is that there is no one to explain that these rappers and singers spend countless hours writing, listening to other artists, perfecting their craft, recording, practicing, and promoting themselves. There are other matters related to celebrities that necessitate long, serious discussions. First, many celebrities create personas that are very different from the people they really are. Even if the image they portray is somewhat true, it is not 100% of who they are. Second, successful rappers and singers (the ones who have the ability to stay in the business for a long time) are intelligent business men. They have a team of competent professionals around them who collaborate with them on matters related to all aspects of their businesses. If they do not have a competent team of legal and accounting professionals, they go bankrupt . . . fast. Third, if the rappers and singers who our young Black boys revere, spent all of their time "popping bottles," having sex, and partying, they would never have time to create and perfect the music that made them famous in the first place (selah).

Black boys also need to know what misogyny is and the irrevocable damage that is done to the Black community when Black females are reduced to being whores (hoes), bitches, and tricks. In order to bring about a positive change, young Black boys need to have meaningful relationships with role models who have healthy families (notice that I did not say perfect families) in which they are actively involved. Black boys who do not have positive role models in their lives, as well as those who do can glean a great deal from being around and watching good African American male teachers. They learn how to dress, how to speak, how to act under pressure, how to be gracious in unflattering situations, how to apologize without groveling, how to be angry but not offensive, how to be kind to people who are not kind to them, how to say just enough, how to laugh, when to code switch, when to argue a point, how to disagree without being disagreeable, how to "play the game," along with countless other lessons of life.

Thorough, articulate, African American male teachers can also engage young Black men who struggle academically. Research suggests that middle-grade-level Black students struggle academically (Gay, 2000; Reynolds, 1999). Those who have raised children through middle school years, teach or serve as administrators in middle schools or work with middle school children know that these years can be tempestuous. Puberty, acne, relationships, identity, hormones, hormones, and more hormones have a profound effect on the development of all middle-grade students, not just African Americans; however, research suggests that academic difficulties experienced by African American students are associated with perceptions of the teacher-student relationship (Ferguson, 2003; Noguera, 2003). The presence of African American male teachers and mentors can have a profound impact on African American male students and their ability to make it through this turbulent time successfully. This topic has such far-reaching implications that it has attracted the attention of our government officials and our President. President Obama has discussed the significance of establishing positive male mentoring programs that promote social identity within the Black community (Noble, 2009).

CHAPTER 6

On the Front Lines

Thomas Whitley, Ph.D.

Dr. Thomas Whitley has been a principal for 17 years. He graduated from Smithfield High School in Smithfield, VA, a rural, working-class town known for pork products. While at Smithfield High, Dr. Whitley, affectionately known as Hawkeye, was a tremendous athlete. He received his Bachelor's degree from Delaware State University in Dover, DE, where he was also a member of the football team. Dr. Whitley received his master's degree from Old Dominion University in Norfolk, VA, and his Ph.D. from Virginia Polytechnic Institute and State University in Blacksburg, VA.

As a student at Smithfield High School, Dr. Whitley was influenced by Joseph Buggs, a teacher and football coach. "Coach Buggs was my football coach at Smithfield High. He had a huge, positive impact on my life. He was the first person, other than my parents, to talk to me about the possibilities of college and that it could become a reality for me. He talked to me about the importance of taking the right courses, goal setting, and deciding what I wanted to do with the rest of my life. He is still a major influence in my life; I met him when I was 15, and now I am 50. Coach Buggs was not only an advocate for me, he went out of his way to ensure that all of his student athletes had the opportunity to receive an education and compete at institutions of higher learning. When it came time for me to visit colleges, Coach Buggs drove me to Delaware State, and I ended up getting a full scholarship. He was a powerful force in my life and the lives of countless other student athletes at Smithfield High School."

When asked about the educational impact that Coach Buggs had on him, Dr. Whitley responded: "The fact that he was an educator and the fact that I always wanted to work with kids had an impact on me. I was uncertain as to a major during my freshman year, so I was undecided during my freshman year. I had the opportunity to work with the National Youth Sports Program. I also worked as a counselor to disabled kids and kids in poverty. During my sophomore year, the light bulb went on as I served as a counselor to these young people. This is when I knew I wanted to teach. I student taught at all levels, elementary through high school. After my various experiences on the different levels, I discovered my passion was high school."

When asked about the impact that thorough, articulate, African American male teachers can have on African American students, Dr. Whitley had the following to say:

"They can have a tremendous impact. African American male teachers, like all teachers, have the power to hurt or heal. In many cases, they serve as role models. So many kids come from broken homes and don't have a positive male in their lives. These kids come to school for structure, security, and encouragement. They come looking to fill a void in their lives. A positive teacher can do this. Teachers never know the impact they have on students. Students may never articulate the impact that educators have on them, but there is no doubt that African American male teachers can and have influenced lives. I never look at myself as a role model, but as a professional, and I take my profession very seriously. I serve as the leader and put myself in the right direction. I can't (in good conscience) put myself in a position where a kid could say I have disappointed him/her. If we can get educators with the same mindset and same vision who are willing to accept that responsibility, we can reduce the crime, gang related issues, and poverty that plague the Black community. We can do this simply by being involved and staying involved in a child's life. The problem is that people say they want to serve as a mentor for a kid, but for how long? You can't be a part-time mentor. You can't be with a kid for 6 months then exit his life forever. People who do that are following the same pattern that they have seen all of their lives. Too many young, Black boys have men who are in their lives for a season then are gone. I met Coach Buggs when I was 15, and I still have a relationship with him at 50. That's a true mentor. Kids need stability and consistency. Thorough, articulate African American male teachers can change the course of society and the direction of education. We can't wait until children get to high school, we must begin to make an impact elementary and middle school. I had both parents, but Coach Buggs was still like a father to me. He even attended my college graduation. So many of our African-American males do not see the genius inside of themselves, and educators can change this."

Chapter 7

Historical Black Teachers and Scholars

The diligent work of Black teachers and scholars has resulted in momentous contributions to society. Accordingly, Black male role models in education have provided pathways and processes that have addressed issues in education, civil rights, medicine, and economics. Collectively, historical Black teachers worked to establish theoretical and practical approaches that influenced American culture by providing their communities with road maps for transforming Black students into productive members of society. These courageous pioneers in the teaching profession have laid unyielding foundations that have facilitated the growth, development, and success of young people of all races.

Booker T. Washington (1856-1915)

In 1881, Booker T. Washington became the president of Tuskegee Institute in Alabama, where he introduced the self-help philosophy coined the Tuskegee model that focused on economic self-reliance and agricultural training and development (Dunn, 1993). Washington's education philosophy affirmed that Black people must learn through experience and develop tools that would solve their own problems (Dunn, 1993;, Gyant. 1998).

Additionally, Washington's (1896, 1904) emphasis on "hand training" affirmed that through *doing* and *experience,* African Americans would have the ability to become self reliant and independent. For that reason, Washington was responsible for educating African Americans and providing guidance that would result in self-reliance. Washington (1896) stated,

The seven millions of colored people of the
South cannot be reached directly by any

mission agency, but they can be reached
by sending out among them strong selected
young men and women, with the proper
training of head, hand, and heart, who will
live among these masses and show them
how to lift themselves up. The problem
that the Tuskegee Institute keeps before
itself constantly is how to prepare these
leaders (p. 2).

Booker T. Washington (1896) believed that
teaching consisted of modeling proper training that
developed skills that encourage self-reliance. Similarly,
students today benefit from the presence of positive
Black male teachers who promote student persistence
and advocate student success.

W.E.B. Du Bois (1868-1963)

In 1902, an article entitled "Of the Training of
Black Men" published in the *Atlantic Monthly* and
later published in the *Souls of Black Folk,* Du Bois
(1902), associated the institution of slavery with the
negative practices and behaviors of Black people.
Du Bois stated, "To stimulate wildly weak and
untrained minds is to play with might fires; to flaunt

their striving idly is to welcome a harvest of brutish crime and shameless lethargy in our very laps. The guiding of thought and the deft coordination of deed is at once the path of honor and humanity" (Du Bois, 1902, p. 2). The condition of Black people required a particular orientation to learning that would assist in their progress (Brown, 2006). Du Bois was a model to students who were literate, well-trained, resourceful, and thoughtful individuals. Du Bois stated, "To-day it is proved by the fact that four hundred Negroes, many of whom have been reported as brilliant students, have received the bachelor's degree from Harvard, Yale, Oberlin, and seventy other leading colleges." He further stated with regard the graduates of these institutions, "nowhere have I met men and women with a broader spirit of helplessness, with deeper devotion to their life work [. . .]" (Du Bois, 1902, p.7). As a result, the "Talented Tenth," which was the philosophy that approximately one-tenth of the Black population should attend elite colleges and would be "entrusted to return to African American communities to educate the masses of their race and ultimately lead the Negro out of economic, political, and social bondage" (p. 29-30). In this context, Du Bois envisioned the Black teacher as a central source of cultural, moral, political, and social knowledge vital to elevating other Black Americans (Brown, 2006).

Carter G. Woodson (1875-1950)

Carter G. Woodson, a teacher and mentor, published his seminal text, *The Mis-education of the Negro,* which evaluated the industrial and classic models of education for Black students. Woodson affirmed that industrialized education did not prepare African American for employment (Brown, 2006). As a result, Woodson (2000 [1933}) scrutinized the inadequacies and addressed the problems in the education or the "mis-education of the Negro." For example, the curriculum in traditional education programs fostered an ideology of inferiority (Woodson, 2000 [1933}). For this reason, Woodson believed that traditional curricula did not complement the intellectual ability of Africans. Woodson (2000 {1933}) here elaborates on this point:

> Students were not told that ancient Africans of the interior knew sufficient science to concoct poisons for arrowheads, to mix durable colors for paintings, to

extract metals from nature and refine them
for development in industrial arts (p. 18).

Woodson (2000 [1933}) further asserted that forms of "mis-education" of African Americans encouraged class differences and community mistrust, which ultimately influenced political and social disruptions in the African American community. Because of the process of mis-education, the African American teacher then became a meaningless icon that had no direct impact on the African American community.

> With "mis-educated Negroes" in control
> themselves, however, it is doubtful that the
> system would be very much different from
> what it is or that it would rapidly undergo
> change. The Negroes thus placed in charge
> would be the products of the same system
> and would show no more conception of
> that task at hand than do the Whites who
> have educated them and shaped their
> minds as they would have then function.
> Negro educators of today may have more
> sympathy and interest in the race than the
> Whites now exploiting Negro institutions
> as educators, but the former have no more

vision than their competitors. Taught
from books of the same bias, trained by
Caucasians of the same prejudices, or by
Negroes of enslaved minds, one generation
after another serves no higher purpose
than to do what they are told to do (p. 23).

Woodson's study outlined the role and expectation of Black teachers. His seminal text, *The Miseducation of the Negro,* questioned the processes of the educational system as well as theorists he called the "hidden curriculum" (Apple, 1975; Giroux, 1983) who were responsible for African American students' education conditions. Woodson (2000 [1933]) believed that in order to correct the dilemma of "miseducation," the re-development of a curriculum would foster the self-worth and racial consciousness of the Black student. According to Woodson (2000 {1933}),

To educate the Negro we must find out
exactly what his background is, what he is
today, what his possibilities are, and how
to begin with him as he is and make him
a better individual of the kind that he is.
Instead of cramming the Negro's mind
with what others have shown that they can

> do, we should develop his latent powers
> that he may perform in society a part
> which others are not capable (p. 151).

Woodson's ideology as outlined in his work, *The Mis-education of the Negro*, addressed issues and identified best practices for educating African Americans.

Ernest Everett Just (1883-1941)

Ernest Everett Just was a true teacher and mentor. As a humble and unassuming scientist at Howard University, Dr. Just employed scientific methods and inquiry to challenge the theories of biologists of the 19th and 20th centuries (Just). Dr. Just served as a professor in the medical school and head of the Department of Physiology where his profound understanding of varied aspects of the cell resulted in his scientific contributions to the process of artificial parthenogenesis and the physiology of cell development (Just).

Dr. Ernest Just was a true teacher and scholar. His mentorship of three undergraduate students at Howard University led to the establishment of Omega Psi Phi Fraternity, Inc. Dr. Just assisted the undergraduate students with their academic, social, professional, and fraternal development much like a parent or big brother would. As a role model, Dr. Just upheld the Cardinal Principles of the Fraternity. Through his own character and actions, he was the highest example of manhood, and he admonished the members of the undergraduate chapter to follow his example. (Chapter Advisor Manual)

As a mentor, Dr. Just stressed the importance of maintaining high scholarship by encouraging the efforts of the brothers to improve scholarship by setting up study groups. Additionally, uplift was exhibited through participation in the fraternity's social action initiative and other activities on and off campus. Dr. Just discharged his responsibility for training the undergraduates in perseverance by keeping before them the importance of developing into well-rounded men and, by example, completing all tasks started; not the least of which for the undergraduate brothers is successfully completing their undergraduate studies and earning a degree (Chapter Advisor Manual).

El-Hajj Malik El-Shabazz (1925-1965)

El-Hajj Malik El-Shabazz, known as Malcolm X, was an African-American Muslim minister, orator, and human rights activist. Malcolm X was also a courageous advocate for human rights and one of the greatest and most influential African Americans in the 20th century. Before his religious conversion and transformation to activism, Malcolm X was incarcerated for a list of crimes. During his incarceration, he met a teacher who is credited with mentoring him. According to *The Autobiography of Malcolm X*, "He [Malcolm X] meets Bimbi, a confident Black prisoner whose speech commands the respect of guards and inmates alike. Under Bimbi's instruction, Malcolm begins to think outside the hustler mindset of his youth. He makes use of the small prison library, refines his English, and channels his rage into reasoned argument" (Haley, 1981).

> Malcolm X did not begin to put time to good use until he was encouraged to do so by Bimbi, an older con who'd spent many years in many prisons but had not wasted his time. Bimbi was articulate and well-read, and he became a minister

to Malcolm, who'd been drawn to Bimbi because 'he was the first man I had ever seen command total respect with his words.' Bimbi reignited within Malcolm the passion for words and the acquisition of knowledge that he'd begun to lose in the 8th grade. He urged Malcolm to take advantage of the prison library, and to enroll in some of the correspondence courses allowed by the prison.

The positive influence of the Black teacher is obvious during the life of Malcolm X. The modeling of strength and discipline enabled Malcolm X to influence the Black community and American history.

Black male teachers, scholars, and activists have made in momentous contributions to society. Accordingly, Black male role models in education have provided pathways and processes that have addressed issues the Black community. These courageous pioneers in the teaching profession have laid unyielding foundations that provide growth, enrichment, and success throughout the Black experience.

Many educational stakeholders recognize the significance of the presence of Black male teachers.

Many historically black colleges and universities (HBCU) play an important role in structuring programs and curricula that develop African American students by harnessing their academic potential to ensure that they achieve learning outcomes (Feagin & Sikes, 1994). For this reason, African American males must be recruited and encouraged to pursue fields in education because there is no substitute for their presence (Boyd & Allen, 1995). A strong male presence within schools will influence school reform that will ultimately benefit Black male students.

Admiration and Respect vs. "Love"

It is important to note here that it is one thing to love a person and another to admire and respect that person. It is easy for children of other races to love a kind, gentle, and witty Black character like Uncle Remus or the character that Morgan Freeman played in Driving Miss Daisy. Black men like that are important, and all people should have a kind, gentle, modest, and meek side; however, we are not aiming for that mark alone when we speak of the kind of Black man we envision in the classroom. Education needs the kind of thorough Black man that children of all races can respect for his kindness, gentleness, modesty, and meekness in addition to his thoroughness, eloquence, and tenacity. Northern Black men are naturally articulate in most cases, so they sound more intelligent. One has to listen closely to how a person uses words in order to determine if that person has truly mastered the language. Phrases like "working to a goal" as opposed to "working toward a goal" and "involved with a process" as opposed to "involved in a process" are sure-fire signs that a person has not mastered the language. Southern Black men have to be more cognizant of their pronunciation than men from other regions of the country. They don't necessarily have to speak like they are from the North or the Midwest, but they certainly have to conquer the traditionally lazy southern tongue. The major thing that Black men have to avoid is errors in subject/verb agreement. Knowing the conventions of the language can mean the difference between having students admire them and having students laugh behind their back. People do not usually correct adults when they speak; they just make mental notes and talk about it later with their friends. It is true that being thorough and articulate don't necessarily make a teacher admirable, but it certainly helps.

The truly thorough Black male has to balance gentleness, modesty, meekness, thoroughness, eloquence, and tenacity in order to be successful. He must balance kindness and sternness, formal language and colloquial language, laughter and gravity. He must also know when to take control and when to relinquish it. He must know when to speak and when to be silent. Of course, most people do not enter education with these qualities, but with the right mentor, almost anyone can learn about the delicate balance that must exist with these personality traits if one intends to get the most out of students and develop relationships that are strong, valuable, and enduring.

CHAPTER 8

Profiles of Men in Education

In examining the importance of African American male teachers, we would be remiss not to include the profiles of some of these heroes on the home front. We have chosen educators with different levels of experience who personify the type of African American male that America's schools need.

Philip Smith, III-retired Health and Physical Education teacher and coach

Hometown:	Newport News, VA
High School Attended:	Huntington High School
Extra-Curr Activities:	Football, track, choir, Student Council, newspaper staff, Motor Club, Industrial Arts Club, yearbook staff, student patrol
HS Graduation:	1955
College(s):	Elizabeth City State University, Hampton University, Old Dominion University
Places Taught:	Westside High School, Smithfield, VA 1961-1969

Denbigh High School,
Newport News, VA
1965-1975
Phoebus High School,
Hampton, VA 1975-1982
Spratley Middle School,
Hampton, VA 1983-1985
Davis Middle School,
Hampton, VA 1986-1991

Activities/sports: Football, wrestling, basketball, track and field

Major accomplishments/honors/awards:

- Holds the record for most touchdowns scored in one season by a player-Huntington High School-1955
- Received an athletic scholarship from Elizabeth City State University-1955
- Led ECSU's football team in rushing yardage-1959
- 5th in the CIAA in rushing yardage-1959
- Named captain of the ECSU Football Team-1961
- Voted Coach of the Year-Westside High School-1955, 1967, 1968
- Won 3 state championships in football
- First Black head coach in the Virginia High School League-1971

- First Black head football coach in Hampton City Public Schools-1975 Phoebus High School
- Honored by former players and students-2011
- Recognized by Hampton City Council-2011
- Recognized by Norfolk State University-2011
- Recipient of the ECSU 60's Decade Image Award
- Recipient of the Down East Sports Gala *Unsung Hero Athletic Award*-2009
- Recipient of the ECSU Alumni Affairs Award-2011
- Charter member of the ECSU Vikings Varsity Club
- Inducted into Elizabeth City State University's Hall of Fame for his accomplishments as a student athlete-2013
- Life member-NAACP
- Life member-ECSU National Alumni Association

Life-Altering Moment: Being hired as the first Black head coach in the Virginia High School League

Philosophy of Education:

"I believe that formal training, along with discipline, whether it's in the academic arena or vocational arena is really the key to a successful life.

If these are mastered, one will be able to provide for himself or herself and his or her family.

Additional Information:

Mr. Smith is an active member of First Baptist Church East End in Newport News, VA. He maintains active memberships and involvement with the National High School Coaches Association, the Hampton Retired Teachers Association, and the Peninsula Chapter of the ECSU National Alumni

Association. He is the benefactor of the Philip Smith, III Scholarship Fund at ECSU. He is married to Raye Smith and the proud father of 2 sons, Philip, IV and Elliott. He has 3 grandchildren, Philip V, Sydney, and Cymphany.

<u>Ronel Brewer</u>

Hometown:	Born in Omaha, Nebraska
	• Pre-K Years on Hahn Air Force Base in Germany
	• Kindergarten through high school in Hampton, Virginia.
High School Attended:	Hampton High School- Hampton, VA 1991-1995
Extra-Curricular Act.—	NAACP, Football, CBAC, Pic Wick, Yearbook, Journalism and School Paper, Kappa Alpha Psi Fraternity Inc., Jazz Band and Marching Band, Theatre, SCA and SGA.
HS Graduation:	1995

College(s):	Elizabeth City State University Norfolk State University
Places Taught:	Virginia Beach Central Academy August 2002-Dec 2009. Renaissance Academy Jan 2010-
Activities/Sports Coached:	Chess Club, sophomore class, Intramurals, Varsity Football, Girls' Varsity Basketball

Major Accomplishments/ Honors/Awards:

- Tagged by the Superintendent 2004
- Reading Teacher of the Year 2011-2012
- Teacher of the Year 2012-2013
- Finalist-Steve Harvey Hoodie Awards 2012

Life-Altering Moment: "My father passed away in 2001. I watched how much he gave the world, and it made me want to give to as many people as I could, as well."

Philosophy of Education:

"I became a teacher due to my desire to help young people to realize their unique ability to learn and be successful. I have always felt the need to be needed. I enjoy teaching others what I know. As a teacher, I have had the opportunity to touch many lives. A great man once told me 'In the field of education, you have the ability to multiply the number of lives you touch.' I have been fortunate enough to be an educator and touch lives for 12 years. As the world changes and children become harder to reach because of antiquated educational practices, my youth has helped me to bridge the gap between the modern day student and education. In my 12 years in the field of education, my intensity to reach students has multiplied. My hunger to guide them towards positive avenues has brought me to a ravenous state of irrepressible determination to make a difference. I feel that this career choice has empowered me to make the vision and goals I have set a reality.

Every child in America has the right to receive a free and appropriate public education. Although this opportunity is afforded to every child, some do not desire to take full advantage of this. I believe every child can learn. I intend on reaching each child with whom I come in contact. I believe that all children have to be empowered with the knowledge and skills necessary to meet the challenges of the future. These skills are not limited to the realm of academia. Appropriate social behavior is also a skill which must be instilled and mastered.

I have had the opportunity to work under four different administrations. This has afforded me the opportunity to see different management styles. This unique opportunity has opened my eyes to the reality of differentiation and the effects that it has on different learners."

Maurice Huff

Hometown:	Norfolk, VA
High School Attended:	Granby High School, Norfolk, VA
Extra-Curricular Act.—	Basketball, football, Honor Society, and Art Club
HS Graduation:	1973
College(s):	Old Dominion University-Norfolk, VA
Places Taught:	Ruffner Middle School (1 year—Student Teaching and Internship), Azalea Gardens Middle School (1 year—Student Teaching & long term volunteer internship),

Presently at Elephant's
Fork Elementary School,
Suffolk, VA

Major accomplishments/honors/awards:

- Rookie Teacher of the Year—Elephant's Fork Elementary School—2002
- Airman of the Year—1980—USAF-Ellsworth AFB

Life-Altering Moment:

"I saw a video at a conference that explained with real life examples that 'Children don't care about what you say until they know you care about them!'"

Philosophy of Education:

"I believe all students are special regardless of race, creed, or color. Their uniqueness is what makes them so special! I also believe that there is a genius within every student. My challenge is to help mold, shape, educate, and motivate the genius in each student.

I believe that 'A student only cares what you know when they honestly know that you care.' Genuine 'care' cannot be feigned or imitated. It must come from the heart. When this authentic love and commitment to the student and the profession is present, it will awaken and invigorate the genius in every student, even the ones who (in the past) may have been dying or suffering in their educational experience.

Finally, I believe that there must be an extraordinary understanding of the value of great classroom management, for without it, even the best and brightest students will demonstrate and show signs of occasional, unacceptable behavior. In contrast, when it (great classroom management) is practiced, expectations rise and students feel safe and at peace, and the educational drive of each begin to soar!!

When students enter my classroom, they walk in to pleasant sounds of instrumental music and a sign that greets them with the uplifting words **'ALL STUDENTS ARE SUPERSTARS!'"**

Conclusion

"High time" is a phrase that means long overdue or about time. In terms of African American/Black men, it is high time for some changes. It is time for African American men to take a more active role in shaping young minds, not just the minds of other Black males but the minds of children of other races. This will not be accomplished by grandiose speeches from lofty pulpits; it will not be accomplished by incessant activism, television and/or radio exposure. The opportunity to shape the lives of the most endangered population in the world exists in the classroom. The most successful "life changers" are men and women who show up to work in schools across the nation with a fervent desire to sow seeds of knowledge, creativity, and intellectual inquiry in the impressionable minds of young scholars.

Each school year can be compared to a journey for teachers and students. Along this journey, there are moments filled with laughter and moments filled with tears. There are times of leisure and times of painstaking work along the journey. There are moments of conflict, anger and resolution along the journey. There are even times when (for whatever reason) people are lost along the way. Throughout this journey, students should be able to count on their teacher to be a model of,

- humility that says, "I can walk with Kings without losing my compassion for the common man,"
- transparency that says, "I make mistakes because I am human, and I will understand your humanity, as well,"
- scholarship that says, "I am a lifelong learner who teaches all and learns from all,"
- fairness that says, "I will ensure that the playing field is level for everyone,"
- dedication that says, "I will not give up on you,"

- tenacity that says, "I will walk with you every step of the way,"
- grace under fire,
- truth.

Imagine . . . just imagine that this educator/ journeyman is an African American man. How many generational stereotypes can be destroyed? How many walls can be torn down? How many lives can be enriched? This is the call for all educators. If these educators happen to be thorough, articulate, Black men, how different would the world be? It is high time that thorough, articulate, African American men join the sojourners on this quest.

WORKS CITED

AFT survey shows teacher pay insufficient. (2007). *American Teacher, 91*(7), 3-3. Retrieved from http://search.proquest.com/docview/217242011?acc ountid=27965

Anderson, Makeebra M. "Why don't Black Men Achieve as Well Academically?" http://www. blackpressusa.com/news/Article.asp?SID=3&T itle=National+News&NewsID=3755. Accessed December 31, 2010.

Are Male Teachers on the Road to Extinction? NEA. 28 April 2004. http://www.nea.org/ newsreleases/2004/nr040428.html Accessed October 11, 2008.

The Autobiography of Malcolm X: As told to Alex Haley (Ballantine Books, 1981). p. 173

Ben Carson. (2013). *The Biography Channel website.* Retrieved 11:00, Apr 06, 2013, from http://www.biography.com/people/ben-carson-475422.

Boyd, H. & Robert, A. (1995). *Brotherman: The Odyssey of Black Men in America—an Anthology.* LOCATION OF PUBLISHER? Ballantine Publishing Group.

Brock, B. L., & Grady, M. I. (1997). *From first year to first-rate: Principals guiding beginning teachers.* Thousand Oaks, CA: Corwin Press.

Brown, Anthony Leroy (2006). Am I my brother's keeper? Examining the political and racial discourses of African American male teachers working with African American male students. Ph.D. dissertation, The University of Wisconsin—Madison, United States—Wisconsin. Retrieved August 22, 2009, from Dissertations & Theses: Full Text. (Publication No. AAT 3234725).

Brown, H. (2001). NBA.com: Michael Jordan career retrospective. *NBA.com: Michael Jordan Career Retrospective.* Retrieved from http://www.nba.com/jordan/hubieonjordan.html

Chmelynski, C. (2006). Getting more men and blacks into teaching. *Education Digest,71*(5), 40-42.

Chideya, F. (January, 1999). *The Color of our future: Our multiracial future.* William Morrow & Co.

Comer, J. P., and A. F. Poussaint. 1992. Raising Black children. New York, NY: Lume.

Cones, J. & White, J. (1999). *Black Man Emerging.* Routledge.

Cornel West. (2013). *The Biography Channel website.* Retrieved 12:49, Apr 07, 2013, from http://www.biography.com/people/cornel-west-9528216.

Cozzens, L. (1998, May 25). *Brown v. board of education* (Rep.). Retrieved March 11, 2013, from http://www.watson.org/~lisa/blackhistory/early-civilrights/brown.html.

Diamond, L. (2011, January 31). Duncan calls on black men to become teachers. *Atlanta Journal-Constitution.* Retrieved June 22, 2011, from http://www.ajc.com/news/news/local/duncan-calls-on-black-men-to-become-teachers/nQqCL/

Dinham, S. (1994, September). *Enhancing the quality of teacher satisfaction.* Paper presented at the National Conference of the Australian College of Education, Launceston, Tasmania, Australia.

Du Bois, W.E.B. (1902). Of training of Black men. *Atlantic Monthly.* Retrieved July 7, 2003. http://

www.theatlantic.com/unbound/flashnks/blacked/
dutrain.htm.

Dunn, F. (1993). The education philosophies of Washington, Du Bois, and Houston: Laying the foundation for Afrocentrism and Multiculturalism. *The Journal of Negro Education, 62* (1), 24-34.

Ferguson, R. F. (2003). Teachers' perceptions and expectations and the Black-White test score gap. *Urban Education, 38*, 460-507.

Gay, G. (2000). *Culturally responsive teaching: Theory, research, and practice.* New York, NY: Teachers College Press.

Grose, T. K. (2006). Poor showing in science and math. *Asee Prism, 15*(9), 22.

Gyant, L. (1988). Contributions to adult education: Booker T. Washington, George Washington Carver, Alain Locke, and Ambrose Caliver. *Journal of Black Studies.* 19 (1), 97-110.

Iaffaldano, M. T., & Muchinsky, P. M. (1985). Job satisfaction and job performance: A meta-analysis. *Psychological Bulletin, 97*(2), 251-273. doi: 10.1037//0033-2909.97.2.251

Ingersoll, R. M. (2001b). The realities if out-of-field teaching. *Educational Leadership, 58*, 42-45.

Irizarry, J. G. (2007). "Home-growing" teachers of color: Lessons learned from a town-gown partnership. *Teacher Education Quarterly*, 88.

Hutchinson, E. (1995). *Black fatherhood: The guide to male parenting.* Los Angeles, CA:

Middle Passage Press.

Hutchinson, E. (1995). *Black fatherhood II: Black women talk about their men.*

Los Angeles, CA: Middle Passage Press.

Hutchinson, E. (1995). *Blacks and reds: Race and class in conflict, 1919-1990.*

Michigan: Michigan State University Press.

Jones, S. (Ed.). (2001, Summer). Teachers as professionals. *Forum on Education*. Retrieved from http://www.aps.org/units/fed/newsletters/summer2001/jones.html

Kelly, J., & Dozier, G. (2010). L. Douglas Wilder. *The Story of Virginia: An American Experience.* Retrieved April 07, 2013, from http://www.vahistorical.org/sva2003/wilder.htm

Kim, J., & Loadman, W. (1994). *Predicting teacher job satisfaction.* Columbus, OH: Ohio State University.

King, S. H. (1993). The limited presence of African American teachers. *Review of Educational Research, 63*(2), 115-149.

Koehler, Paul and Lewis, Joy. Criticism of Public Education. The Gale Group. 2009. Accessed December 27, 2010 from http://www.education.com/reference/article/public-education-criticism-of/.

Kunjufu, J. (2005). *Countering the conspiracy to destroy black boys.* Chicago, IL: African American Images.

Ladson-Billings. (1994). *Dreamkeepers: Successful teachers of African American children.* San Francisco, CA: Jossey-Bass.

Landsberger, H. A. (1979). *Hawthorne revisited.* Ithaca, NY: W.F. Humphrey.

Lee, C. (1991). *Empowering Young Black Males.* Clearinghouse on Counseling and Personnel Services Ann Arbor MI, ERIC Identifier: ED341887.

Levinson, E. M., Fetchkan, R., & Hohenshil, T. (1988). Job satisfaction among practicing school psychologists revisited. *School Psychology Review, 17,* 101-111.

Lewis, C. (2002). *Lesson study: A handbook of teacher-led instructional change.* Philadelphia, PA: Research for Better Schools.

Lewis, M. (2005, March 14). "Call me MISTER program seeks to increase recruitment of Black men for teachers." Retrieved from http://www.blackamericaweb.com/site.aspx/bawnews/mister315

Lynch, M., & Carr, H. (2006). *Closing the racial academic achievement gap.* Chicago, IL: African American Images.

Marston, S. H., Brunetti, G. J., & Courtney, V. B. (2005). Elementary and high school teachers: Birds of a feather? *Education, 125*(3), 469-495.

Marston, S., Courtney, V., & Brunetti, G. (spring 2006). The voices of experienced elementry teachers: Their insights about the profession. *Teacher Education Quarterly. 33*(2), 111-132.

Milloy, C. (2013, February 19). National percentages of black male teachers and administrators are extremely low. Explore common problems and common sense solutions regarding poor performance of black boys in American schools. *Washington Post.*

Nelson, B. G. (2002, November). The importance of men teachers and reasons why there are so few a survey of members NAEYC Bryan G. Nelson. *The Importance of Men Teachers and Reasons Why There Are so Few (Open Library).* Retrieved from http://openlibrary.org/books/OL19688035M/

The_importance_of_men_teachers_and_reasons_ why_there_are_so_few

New Georgia Encyclopedia: Andrew Young (b. 1932). (n.d.). In *New Georgia Encyclopedia: Andrew Young (b. 1932)*. Retrieved from http://www. georgiaencyclopedia.org/nge/Article.jsp?id=h-1395

Noble, D. (2009). *Impressions of Black leadership as informed by the presidential candidacy of Barack Obama: A case stud*. University of Nebraska— Lincoln 281 pages

Noguera, P. A. (2003). The trouble with Black boys: The role and influence of environmental and cultural factors on the academic performance of African American males. *Urban Education*, (38), 431-459.

Omega Psi Phi Fraternity http://www.getinvolved. purdue.edu/Community?action=getOrgHome&or gID=322

Pearson, L. C., & Moomaw, W. (2005). The relationship between teacher autonomy and stress, work satisfaction, empowerment, and professionalism. *Educational Research Quarterly*, *29*, 37-54.

Quinn, R., & Andrews, B. (2004). The struggles of first-year teachers: Investigating support mechanisms. *The Clearing House, 77*(4), 164-169.

Reber, S. J. (2005). Court ordered segregation: Successes and failures integrating American schools since Brown versus board of education. *Journal of Human Resources,40*(3), 559-590. Retrieved May 30, 2011, from http://www.jstor.org/stable/4129552

Reynolds, A. & Gill, S. (1999). Educational expectations and school achievement of urban African American children. *Journal of School Psychology*, (37), 403-424.

Richards, J. (2004). What new teachers value most in principals. *Principal Magazine, 63*(3), 42-44.

Russell Simmons. (2013). *The Biography Channel website*. Retrieved 12:01, Apr 07, 2013, from http://www.biography.com/people/russell-simmons-307186.

Sargent, T., & Hannum, E. (2005). Keeping teachers happy: Job satisfaction among primary school teachers in rural northwest China. *Comparative Education Review, 49*(2), 173-206. Retrieved from http://eric.ed.gov/ERICWebPortal/recordDetail?accno=EJ725138

Shann, M. (1998). Professional commitment and satisfaction among teachers in urban middle scools. *The Journal of Education Research, 92*(2), 67-73.

"Shortage of Male Teachers Worsens in Elementaries-Stereotypes Add to the Imbalance." *The Courier Journal*. Gender Public Advocacy Coalition. 24 November 2004.

Spector, P. E. (1997). *Job satisfaction: Application, assessment, causes, and consequences*. Thousand Oaks, CA: Sage.

Staples, R. (1989). *The Black American family*. In C. Mindel et al.(eds.), *Ethnic Families in America: Patterns and Variations*. New York: Elsevier North Holland, Inc. Smith, Jessie Carney.

Swift, M. (2007, March 12). Divided by gender. *San Jose Mercury News (CA)*, p. 1A.

Textiera, E. (2006, July 1). Black men combating stereotypes. *The Washington Post*. Retrieved from http://www.washingtonpost.com/wp-dyn/content/article/2006/07/01/AR2006070100462.html

Thornton, M., & Bricheno, P. (2008). Entrances and exits: Changing perceptions of primary teaching as a career for men. *Early Child Development and Care*, *178*(7), 717-731. doi: 10.1080/03004430802352087

Toppo, G. (2003, July 2). The face of the American teacher; white and female while her students are ethnically diverse. USA Today. Retrieved from

http://www.learningworksca.org/wp-content/
uploads/2012/02/Face-of-American-teachers.pdf

Swift, Mike. "Divided by Gender." San Jose Mercury News (CA). March 12, 2007.

Vancil, M. (1991, December). Michael Jordan: Phenomenon. *NBA.com: Michael Jordan Career Retrospective.* Retrieved December 09, 2008, from http://www.nba.com/jordan/hoop_phenomenon. html

VanVoorhis, R. W., & Levinson, E. M. (2006). Job Satisfaction Among School Psychologists: A Meta-Analysis. *School Psychology Quarterly, 21*(1), 77-90. doi: 10.1521/scpq.2006.21.1.77

Washington, B.T. (1896). The awakening of the Negro. *Atlantic Monthly.* Retrieved July 7, 2003. http://www.theatlantic.com/unbound/flashnks/blacked/washaw.htm.

Woodson, C. G. (2000 [1933]). *The mis-education of the Negro.* Chicago, IL: African American Images.